IT'S A **HEART** THING

"Once you accept Christ, you now have been seated with Him. Now that you're in that position, you purposely do the will of God."

ROSEMARY CANTU

WESTBOW
PRESS®
A DIVISION OF THOMAS NELSON
& ZONDERVAN

WestBow Press books may be ordered through booksellers or by contacting:

WestBow Press
A Division of Thomas Nelson & Zondervan
1663 Liberty Drive
Bloomington, IN 47403
www.westbowpress.com
844-714-3454

Editor: Ryan Singh Paul

ISBN: 978-1-6642-3812-1 (sc)
ISBN: 978-1-6642-3811-4 (hc)
ISBN: 978-1-6642-3813-8 (e)

Library of Congress Control Number: 2021912735

Print information available on the last page.

WestBow Press rev. date: 7/14/2021

CONTENTS

1 JOHN 4:10 THIS IS REAL LOVE—
NOT THAT WE LOVED GOD, BUT
THAT HE LOVED US AND SENT
HIS SON AS A SACRIFICE TO TAKE
AWAY OUR SINS.

OUR BEGINNING IS NOT IN
OUR FALLEN STATE OF SIN. OUR
BEGINNING IS IN THE HEART
OF A LOVING FATHER. THIS IS
THE FOUNDATION OF TRUE
FELLOWSHIP WITH GOD.

MICHAEL OTT MINISTRIES

1

⟨♡⟩

FOCUS ON THE SHINE OF CHRIST

For to set the mind on the flesh is death, but to set the mind on the Spirit is life and peace.
Romans 8:6

When I was growing up, Saturdays were our cleaning days at home. It could be a particularly dreadful day. Certain times during the year, my mother would gather all the brass items and place them together. I remember her laying out newspapers on the living room floor in preparation for my sister and me to start our work. At that moment, I knew it was time for some hideous work. Mom would gather all the brass objects, the oil can, and lots of cloths then hand them to us. We polished until we could see our reflections, otherwise we would have to do it again. After rubbing for what seemed like hours, my shoulders and arms were sore.

I wish I could say there was a reward for us afterward, but the only reward was seeing the tarnished brass come to life. I guess you can say that seeing the hard work pay off did give me a little gratitude.

This is what it is like when we continue to grow in Christ. By living out our true identity in him, more of His truth is exposed. As I think about my inner being, I am excited to know that I become more like Christ the more time I spend with him. God's Word says that as we walk the path of the just, His light will radiate brighter and brighter. His light grows until the perfect day when the saints unite with Christ at His coming. When we continue in His Word, purifying our hearts, the glory of God radiates from us so others can see Him in us. Contrary to what most believe, God does not impose *His will* on humans. He works through the inner self of those who live by and in faith. If God wanted to force His will on humans, then He would not want a relationship with us, and He would not set guidelines for us as Christians. Just a snap of His fingers, and His will would be done in our lives. All God needs to do is speak the word He wants us to do, and *bam*, it is done. Fortunately, that is not how God works. He is fair and just.

> **"My son, be attentive to my words; incline your ear to my sayings.... Let your eyes look directly forward, and your gaze be straight before you."**
>
> **Proverbs 4:20, 25**

Our heavenly Father teaches us to focus on Him and to listen to His words. Why does He tell us not to look to our left or right at the things around us? We have been taught to always be aware of our surroundings so that we will not be knocked down by unwelcome surprises. But living a Christian life is not the same as driving a car where we have to be aware of all four sides. Because we are God's, it is the dark realm who we should always be on the lookout. If someone is walking in darkness, then how can they out walk those who radiate in the light of Jesus?

"Ponder the path of your feet; then all your ways will be sure. Do not swerve to the right or to the left; turn your foot away from evil."
Proverbs 4:25–26

Is God warning us to always be aware of our surroundings? No! Have you ever been in a situation where you needed to put all your attention on what was in front of you because your life depended on it? I vividly remember the night when I walked out of my junior college class, frightened to drive home. I was eighteen and living with my mom and dad. We lived in the next town, which was only about twenty minutes over the harbor bridge from the school. The bridge served as a port with a 138-foot drop, and crossing the bridge was the only way to get to my hometown.

I was taking night classes, and that night it was dark with heavy rain showers. I knew the drive home would be quite stressful. As I turned on the car, I realized that the windshield wipers were not working. As I pulled onto the freeway, I started crying and begging God to help me make it home. At this point in my life I did not know anything about Christianity except the basics the Baptists taught. I slowly made it to the base of the harbor bridge. I headed up, terrified to go any farther, blinded by rain and darkness. Going slowly at about 15 mph, I decided to stay in the middle lane since I was able to see the reflectors on the road. This would help guide me over the bridge. As the heavy rain splattered across the road, rolling down the windshield, panic arose in the pit of my stomach. It felt as if I was the only one on the road and I was terrified. I was not even aware of other cars around me, I was so busy concentrating on the road ahead. I did not realize how tight my hands were gripping the wheel until they began to ache later that night.

When the reflectors came to an end, I had to rely on the painted lines to guide me the rest of the way home. I cried throughout my drive, but I knew that I had to focus on the road ahead of me. I never dared to change lanes, afraid I would be slammed into the cement blocks on my left or bumped over the bridge to my right. All my attention was on staying centered and keeping my eyes forward. Thanks to the Lord, I got home safely. That is one scary night I'll always remember.

When we try to solve a problem happening in our lives, we put so much of our attention on the problem. We become emotionally involved, and if we face difficulties our minds tell us that there is no hope. That distraction takes our focus off God, and this will eventually cause us to fall. There will always be masses of distractions in your life *if* you try to juggle everything on your own. God the Father has this great idea that when His children focus forward, setting their gaze on Him, then and only then can He guide them in life. He never intended for us to live our lives alone. Jesus Christ is our path to freedom. Many times, His Word warns us not to go by what we see: "We walk by faith, not by sight." (2 Cor 5:7). Let his words be a command that overpowers your perceptions. You will always notice lots of negativity in life but turn your eyes to the Word of life. Doing this should be a natural way to live instead of having to *try*. If you have to try to be a good Christian, then it has become more of an effort. In other words, this is what God calls "works." We must reprogram our minds by rewiring our thoughts to be like Christ's. Start opening your heart to a relationship with Christ. During your next fiasco, focus on speaking to Him with a calm heart, avoiding emotional chaos and doubt. Become a victory warrior!

You need to focus on right now, today. A faithful life requires more than just attending church and reading the Bible occasionally. A disciple who loves Christ Jesus is constantly connected to Him. If you try to be the best person on your own, then you are depending on your goodness and not God's. This is what religion is, but a relationship is a spiritual bond from your heart to His. As the saying goes, "The proof is in the pudding." So, the proof of your intimate relationship with Christ is His radiant light shining from the inside out to where others will see Him in you. As illustrated in the polishing of tarnished brass, the love for Christ shines brighter when we die daily to Him. He wants a genuine relationship with you. As disciples, we represent God on earth, just as Christ represented God in the flesh. Sometimes when I speak to others about Jesus, they have their eyes fixed on me. At some point in our conversation, they will say, "I can see Him in your eyes!" or "I see a light around you! You do know Him!" I mention this to show you the power of God! He wants everyone to know Him by revealing Himself through us to others. Our heavenly Father asks us to continue in His Word, purifying our hearts.

A king who sits on a throne would not dress poorly or work in the fields as an ordinary citizen. Neither would his servant take the role of the king in a palace. It just would not make sense. Yet as children of God, we do not live to the full maturity of sons and daughters as His offspring. His children continue to look at life the way the world sees it. "I am unworthy, but thanks be to God." Or many say, "Once you hit a certain age, your body starts breaking down little by little." That is not what Jesus taught, so why do we speak or take in this hellish talk? According to God, true believers are called righteous and holy. Why would any Christian want less and settle for a weak foundation? God has repeated in His Word, warning us not to go by what we see, feel, hear, or touch. One night as I was sleeping, the Lord spoke to me and said, "Stop going by your senses, but live through faith." Immediately I got up to study His Word, and the Spirit lead me to His teachings on faith.

When you look around going about your daily business, your eyes <u>observe everything</u>. Your mind programs the images you see to create meaning. For example, as a baby I had a bottle that used to hold honey. This bottle was in the form of a bear. Today, I have an empty plastic bear container that I kept after taking out the honey. The meaning of it is very sentimental to me.

As you look around, kill your thoughts of negativity. Bring your eyes back to His Word and focus on the truth of God. Lay your eyes on the Word of Life, always. This is why Christ says to walk by faith. You see something bad, scary, or maybe unbeatable, and then you become lost. You feel defeated before the game has even started. You have allowed fear to take over. Your words will speak only what is in your heart. Speak the words that will defeat whatever is going against you.

> **"The good person out of the good treasure of his heart produces good, and the evil person out of his evil treasure produces evil, for *out of the abundance of the heart, the mouth speaks.*"**
> **Luke 6:45**

"Therefore, whoever desires to love life and see good days, let him keep his tongue from evil and his lips from speaking deceit;
let him turn away from evil and do good;
let him seek peace and pursue it.
For the eyes of the Lord are on the righteous, and his ears are open to their prayer. But the face of the Lord is against those who do evil."

1 Peter 3:10-12

Quotes: Truth Be Told …

"SO MUCH OF WHO YOU REALLY
ARE, IS NOT WHO YOU WERE BUT
WHO YOU HAVE BECOME."

ROSEMARY V. CANTU

2

CONSCIOUS RIGHTEOUSNESS

"But the path of the righteous is like the light
of dawn, which shines brighter and brighter
until full day."

Proverbs 4:18

Who Are You Really? If you confess that Christ Jesus is the Son of God and your Savior, then you are worth more than just a job title. Are you a custodian who cleans for a living? Are you a lawyer who seeks justice for others? You may be a custodian as an occupation, but you have Jesus dwelling within you. It is Jesus living in you that makes you who you truly are. When you are born again, you demonstrate your faith by confessing that Jesus is your Lord. This is who you are now: the child of the Most High God, your Father, and sibling to Jesus our Lord. A job title does not define who you are. God's thoughts of you are the truth of the real you.

"For I know the plans I have for you, declares the LORD, plans for welfare and not for evil, to give you a future and a hope."
Jeremiah 29:11

This simply means that our Heavenly Father loves all His children with the same perfect love. No one is more important than another. It takes someone without the wisdom of God to point out the weaknesses in others. Many times, I have heard someone say, "So-and-so person is so spiritual since he speaks into our lives and it comes to pass." Such comments improperly praise man and not the Lord. It is okay to acknowledge another person's gift, since it cannot be denied, but your excitement needs to be for God. It is God's Spirit who works through those given gifts. There is a big difference between glorifying man versus glorifying God. A person who walks in the Spirit walks with the Lord, therefore the Spirt is doing God's work inside their heart. This is when you should glorify God for revealing Himself to you through another. An individual should never be praised as if it is through their own doing. Let us always keep our focus on Christ and His blessings that pour out through other people.

As a side note, we are used to speaking to a congregation of believers, but remember to speak as if unbelievers were (and are) listening, too. Otherwise, unbelievers will assume they fall in the same category as believers. For example, "Let us thank God for finding favor in our lives. We are holy and blameless in His eyes! Amen." A homosexual, cult members, haters of their enemies, etc. may assume they are part of the Body of Christ and take that statement to heart, even though they have not repented. Therefore, always include, "Those who are saved, are a new creation in Christ, then this message pertains to you." Making such a bold statement should have the congregation asking themselves if they are true believers. In a more informal gathering of only a few people, the same rule still applies. Our spiritual focus needs to be spiritual thinking; therefore, we should not prevent others from hearing the Truth due to the fear of stepping on toes.

I. Let us now talk about the lawyer aspect. Lawyers contest cases on behalf of those who need to be represented. A person will stand trial for a wrong which was committed, hoping the representing attorney will argue a winning case. Some lawyers will defend your case regardless of whether they believe in your innocence or not.

Now, here is the point I wish to make. One day as I was reading a book for my Criminal Justice class, the Holy Spirit showed me the power of God's plan to destroy the devil's work.

When a crime is committed, the first question that the

justice system asks is not what type of crime was committed, but where it was committed. The most significant point when in question a crime has been reported is in what geographical jurisdiction was the crime committed? Jurisdiction is very important, since it determines who will investigate, and which court will hold the trial. The crime must be tried under that particular jurisdiction's law.

For example: "Eight men try to rob a racetrack in Illinois, but are thwarted by security guards. In their subsequent prosecution for attempted robbery, they argue that the federal government doesn't have jurisdiction to prosecute them because the alleged crime occurred on state grounds. But because the racetrack's money is federally insured, many of the horses' owners come from out of state, and the track uses several out-of-state services (for betting machines and advertising materials, for example), jurisdiction was properly vested in the U.S. government." (Micah Schwartzbach, Attorney; Nolo.com)

The Lord revealed to me the importance of jurisdiction in our lives. The same concept applies in His plan for our redemption and how it defeats Satan's tactics. The earth and the heavens are God's creation; therefore, the jurisdiction of the entire globe and beyond belongs to Him. When Christ resurrected from the dead and took back the Keys of the Kingdom from Satan, the battle was over, and Satan was defeated. Our Spirit is under God's jurisdiction. Therefore, evil cannot enter unless we let our guard down.

Acknowledging Christ as the Son of God and being filled with the Holy Spirit empowers us to rise in power, authority, and dominion, enabling us to do the works of Christ and more. Those who have died to Christ have become joined with God.

> **"But to all who did receive him, who believed in his name, he gave the right to become children of God ..."**
>
> **John 1:12.**

In our heart resides the Holy Spirt of God. What does this mean? You are God's property; therefore, God has full jurisdiction over you! Satan no longer has the authority to claim you. Now that we have received our dominion back which was lost at the fall of man, we have been given authority, dominion, and power on earth!

> **"I will give you the keys of the kingdom of heaven, and whatever you bind on earth shall be bound in heaven, and whatever you loose on earth shall be loosed in heaven."**
>
> **Matthew 16:19**

This now authorizes Jesus Christ to have full claim on earth as His jurisdiction. Our Lord left His kingdom in Heaven to conquer the devil's playground on earth so that we can live as conquerors with Christ.

"He disarmed the rulers and authorities and put them to open shame, by triumphing over them in him."

Col 2:17

Jesus who lives in you has now overcome the old laws (Moses's laws under the old covenant) and has blessed you under a new covenant. "And be found in Him, not having a righteousness of my own that comes from the law, but that which comes through faith in Christ, the righteousness from God that depends on faith." (Phil 3:9). Therefore, you are justified, righteous, holy, and redeemed because Christ is in you! You now belong to the one and only Christ! **"I thank you Father for you have given them to me, and no one can take them from me."** (John 10:29). Amen, Jesus represents us and will be with us on judgement day. Saying rituals, long prayers, lighting candles and numerous of other things to be heard by God is forbidden by Him. He demands that He be your only God, and there is only one way to Him. The true way is through Jesus Christ our Savior.

⤳

"You shall not make for yourself a carved image, or any likeness of anything that is in heaven above, or that is in the earth beneath, or that is in the water under the earth. You

**shall not bow down to them or serve them, for
I the LORD your God am a jealous God..."**
Exodus 20:4-5

II. If you keep looking at life through your eyes, you will never escape condemnation. How many times have you said something that you regret? Guilt weighs you down, leaving you to beg God for forgiveness. You become very angry with yourself and that can be overwhelming. That is condemnation and according to God,

**"There is therefore now NO condemnation for
those who are in Christ Jesus."**
Romans 8:1

This in no way means to continue in sin, NOR does it mean if you sin you simply shake it off. Yes, there are many pastors who say not to feel condemned, or that there is no need to ask for forgiveness since it has been granted. Although this is true, you should ask yourself, "With what kind of attitude do I have towards Christ? Is there love in my 'I'm forgiven already' attitude?"

As I was speaking with the Lord, questioning why some of his people have no remorse even after they have sinned, He answered, "Just as there are children who take advantage of what their parents do for them, yet others are naturally thankful; so are the children of God." Our Father has children that have a cocky "righteous" attitude, as well as those who have a soft, respectful heart towards Him. Personally, I know when I do something wrong that is out of character to God. I humbly thank Him for forgiving me and I apologize for what I have done. A Christian who says, "I can take what I want (spiritually blessings) because I'm the child of a King," behaves like a spoiled child and does not understand respect, honor, or love towards God. Our Father deserves spiritual worship, which includes a humble heart. Spiritual worship is not about singing, but about having a joyful, loving heart set on fire for God.

> **"I appeal to you therefore, brothers, by the mercies of God, to present your bodies as a living sacrifice, holy and acceptable to God, which *is* your spiritual worship."**
> **Romans 12:1**

A sincere, loving heart is not something that can be taught. This is an emotion living within a person. A person who is not sensitive to their emotions for compassion can still embrace a love lesson from Christ. He teaches love because He is Love. This is the best and most important attribute God expresses in Himself.

> **"Love one another with brotherly affection. Outdo one another in showing honor."**
> **Romans 12:10**

We first need to demonstrate honor towards our Father in heaven. **"Enter his gates with thanksgiving, and his courts with praise! Give thanks to Him; bless His name!" Psalms 100:4**

If we do not show reverence to the One True God, then how can we uphold those higher than ourselves? We are to be servants for others: for those who have not found Jesus, and for our own Christian brothers and sisters. If you are saved by grace through faith and Jesus lives in you, then you are one with Christ. You have a new Spirit. That is the spirit where you live from.

> **"In him you also, when you heard the word of truth, the gospel of your salvation, and believed in him, were sealed with the promised Holy Spirit, who is the guarantee of our inheritance until we acquire possession of it, to the praise of his glory."**
>
> **Ephesians 1:13-14**

Let us look at it from another angle. When you were a sinner doing everything you wanted to do (which is fulfilling the flesh) you were at this time a child of the devil according to Jesus in 1 John 3:9-10: **"By this it is evident who are the children of God, and who are the children of the devil: whoever does not practice righteousness is not of God, nor is the one who does not love his brother."** God is light, and Satan is darkness. Now that you are a child of God, you are the light for Christ. You cannot separate the Truth any more than you can separate Kool-Aid powder from the water once combined. You are complete and one in Him. Jesus who is the Father of Love living in you enables you to love everyone without excuse. If you do not do so, it is not the fault of the offender but yours. Love lives inside you. It is a matter of dying to who you still think you are, so you can live as Christ.

IF **NEVER** IS PART OF YOUR
LANGUAGE TO GROW, THEN YOU
WILL **ALWAYS** BE A PART OF FEAR
TO CHANGE.

———————

ROSEMARY V. CANTU

3

LOVE SHINES
THROUGH MERCY

**"I have been crucified with Christ. It is no
longer I who lives, but Christ who lives in me."**
Galatians 2:20

Many people know of the baptism of Jesus Christ, but how
many have heard of Baptism in the Holy Spirit? God has put
more into his plan for us to be filled with Himself, which
includes another baptism.

> **"And he said to them, "Did you receive the
> Holy Spirit when you believed?" And they
> said, "No, we have not even heard that there
> is a Holy Spirit." And he said, "Into what then
> were you baptized?" They said, "Into John's
> baptism."**
> **Acts 19:2-3**

In John 16:23, Jesus says, "In that day you will ask nothing of me. Truly, truly, I say to you, whatever you ask of the Father in my name, he will give it to you." This was an awesome scripture for me to study. My heart felt bubbly inside, and it seemed to skip a beat or two upon hearing the revelation of this scripture!

Jesus says do not ask anything from <u>Him</u>, but ask his father in His name, Jesus. Christ explains this because He has made **All Things New**! He has done everything in His awesome power to give us His being. He cannot come down from heaven to be crucified again so you can have peace or health or happiness. **"By this, is love perfected with us, so that we may have confidence for the day of judgment, <u>because as he is so also are we in this world.</u>"** (1 John 4:17). We are complete in Him. God is Love, and Love (God) dwells in us, so now we can truly Love.

It was shocking for me the first time I heard from another Christian that since God lives in us, we can experience His full being without effort on our part. In other words, we do not have to love others because God who is Love is already living in us. That is like saying since Jesus was whipped for our sicknesses and diseases, taking it all on himself, we are automatically healed. Yet, God says that with faith, our healing comes. This is actually the influence of New Age thinking on Christianity. New Age believe that if we realize our relationship with God then we can become gods, and we can hold truth to our own value and be filled with all knowledge. We can agree that God is all-knowing, but Christians are not. He is the creator and master of every living and non-living entity. Would you put yourself in His category and proclaim that because God lives inside you, you now are equal in Knowledge? Absolutely not. If this statement was true, then why study His Words and pray? Making a statement like that promotes yourself to a level of godlike-being. As silly as that statement sounds, it should cause the same reaction when a Christian says that because the God of love lives inside them, then they automatically walk in love.

Once you were baptized in the name of Jesus Christ, you transformed into a new being. You must no longer walk in the futile ways of your old thinking. You have been given a new heart and a new mind in Christ. It seems that being baptized to receive salvation is the stopping point for many Christians who are unwilling to undergo any further changes. Jesus gave His life so we can live as soldiers for God. If we are to be "more than conquerors in Christ," then we should be fighting spiritual battles. Thank God our fight is spiritual, which means we have been adopted into the winning kingdom. The resurrection of Christ disarmed the devil, Amen!

> **"He disarmed the rulers and authorities and put them to open shame, by triumphing over them in him."**
>
> **Colossians 2:15**

Love is a gift of God for us, and because of Him, we can love ourselves and others. I have noticed a pattern in some Christians' concept of love. One Sunday, a pastor said during his sermon that "if God is love, then we are automatically walking in love. We may not feel love towards others, but the love for them is there." This statement makes no sense to me, and it does not follow God's teachings. Someone who thinks this way is often not considered a people-person or has a hard time with others in general, so they use God's love as an excuse not to change their ways. Some excuses are:

"I love everyone, but I don't have to show it."

"People get on my nerves, so I ignore them."

"I don't love them, but I like them." Or "God never said I had to love them near, so I'll love them from a distance."

"I'm not a people-person, and God knows this."

There are many other excuses to suit an individual's perspective on love. Try to imagine if Jesus approached you. What if He felt a bad vibe coming from you and then just thought to Himself, "I'll just avoid him and like him from a distance." That sounds awful and unholy, right? As Christians, those negative words should never enter our hearts either.

What does it mean when we pray for people, preach a good word, or feed the homeless because they are the right things to do? These are merely actions unless the Holy Spirit wills you and the deed is done with love. The statement "merely actions" may sound like it contradicts the Bible, since Jesus said to feed the hungry, clothe the naked, and more; but He said to do it with **all your heart** and be led by the spirit.

"But grow in the grace and knowledge of our Lord and Savior Jesus Christ."
2 Peter 3:18.

The same concept applies to Love. Love is a gift from God. If love were automatically in our hearts, Jesus would not have been so adamant about showing love to others. He gave us many examples of how to show love: prayer, forgiveness, helping others, etc.

"Let all that you do be done in love."
1 Corinthians 16:14

Have you ever volunteered to help at your church or lent a hand to someone in need while feeling a little uneasy? Please do not confuse your emotions of "have to," "need to," "have time to," or "feel good about" with the **desire to show love.** God's love overtakes your heart and compels you to do His will for others **only** when you submit to Him. Your fruits will show during these times.

When I was in downtown Dallas, Texas, feeding the homeless with a group from church, there were tremendous of unknown blessings to come. My purpose was not just to feed the homeless and try to save them. I simply approached them as if they were my friends. (This outgoing personality magnified quite a bit when Christ invaded my heart.)

I had a conversation with a gentleman standing next to his basket. As we spoke, he asked me about my belief in God. He asked why I believe in a "nonexistent" God? I answered him, and he continued to ask more questions as he became more irritable. He became upset and started making ugly statements, putting God down and using His name in vain. I angrily said, "Shut your mouth in the name of Jesus! He is my Father whom you are talking about. God loves you regardless of how you feel about Him!" His face went from agitation to fear. (I do not recommend for you to speak to others like this unless The Holy Spirit is speaking to you.) My anger was not from the flesh; it was a righteous anger from love. This atheist apologized and said, "You really do know Him. I'll listen to what you have to say." By the time I was through, he came to believe the existence of God. The seed of Love was planted in his heart that day. I guarantee that if the anger had come from my flesh, he would have known and reacted differently. Everything I do is with real love and compassion. This is not socially learned behavior.

It must be rooted in the heart, sown by Christ in the Spirit. My ministry quote says it all: **Changing hearts, changes minds.**

> **"We continually ask God to fill you with the knowledge of His will through all the wisdom and understanding that the Spirit gives, so that you may live a life worthy of the Lord and please him in every way: bearing fruit in every good work, growing in the knowledge of God, being strengthened with all power according to his glorious might so that you may have great endurance and patience, and giving joyful thanks to the Father, who has qualified you to share in the inheritance of His holy people in the kingdom of light."**
>
> **Colossians 1:9-12**

It should be second nature for your spirit to see others through the eyes of Christ. He is always telling me of others and sharing their hearts with me. He feels so much love for you and everyone in existence. I will never forget the year 2008, when I spoke to the Lord about love. I am a very approachable person, and very much attracted to people, so by no means was love a problem for me, yet I wanted to know how God loved the way He does.

One special day, while alone in my room, I conversed with God. I asked him to show me His love and to pour it into my heart. I was not expecting him to show me at that very moment. I got up to leave my room, and as I was reaching for the door, suddenly God showed up! Instantly, He asked me, "Are you ready?" Somehow my spirit knew exactly what He was asking. I said, "Yes Lord." I went from standing next to my dresser with my hand reaching for the door, to immediately being weighed down to the floor on my knees within seconds. As God was pouring his love into my heart, I began to cry. His love was enormous, and unexplainable. It was a tangible love, not just a feeling.

Suddenly, in a vision, God took me just far enough into heaven where I was able to view Earth. I was standing in the heavens, yet I could see every detail on Earth. God first showed me a beautiful vision of people walking down busy streets, and then He drew me back to reveal the whole Earth once more. The view did not show water and land, but only people. The Lord pointed out to me that every person on Earth was loved by Him, no exceptions. I cried and begged Him, "Lord stop!" During this vision, He was still releasing love within me. I asked Him to pull back His love from me because God's holiness was unbearable. His love was way too much for me to contain! God removed His love just as fast as He had shared it. The love of God had literally held me down to the floor. When He pulled back, he said, "That's how much I love the world, and you." His love is overpowering! This description is the best way I can describe my encounter with Him. It is hard for me to describe the moment. When

I finally stood up, He also showed me a vision of Jesus's beating and His crucifixion. It is no wonder that He finished the will of God because of the love He has for you.

> *"For God so loved the world, he gave his only begotten son ..."*
> **John 3:16.**

Our God is so merciful, and His love is like no other. A couple of years later after my experience with the power of Love, I was driving to pick up my kids from school. During my conversation with the Lord, I thanked Him for the loving relationship He has with me. Then He asked again, as if picking up from our last conversation two years prior, "Are you ready now?" Once again, my spirit knew what the Lord was talking about; our minds were one. (This is an example of what having the mind of Christ means and being one with Him is like.) I grew eager since I knew I had grown up spiritually, so I answered, "Yes, I am." And *bam*, He did it again! At that very moment, my eyes opened to a completely new revelation of love. The love that poured within me showed me a new meaning for love. Every pedestrian walking by, everyone driving in other cars, and anyone else my eyes saw — my heart overflowed with love for them. I wanted to pull over and hug every single one of them. I wanted to tell them how much they are loved by me and by Christ. It was an overflowing of compassion and mercy to understand God's love for them. No impurity, no unworthiness, no discrimination of any sort was judged. Seeing them through the eyes of Christ Jesus and the love of our Father established my firm belief that God is a righteous judge.

> **"If I speak in the tongues of men or of angels, but do not have love, I am only a resounding gong or a clanging cymbal. If I have the gift of prophecy and can fathom all mysteries and all knowledge, and if I have a faith that can move mountains, but do not have love, I am nothing. If I give all I possess to the poor and give over my body to hardship that I may boast, but do not have love, I gain nothing."**
> **1 Corinthians 13:1-3**

I believe a person knows when they love from their heart, or when the words "I love you" are sincere. The same is true for the recipient distinguishing genuine love. It is an intense, warm feeling of reward when people are presented with love. Babies are good at picking up on this. They cry when held by a person who is not "thrilled" to be holding him/her; they can feel the "bad vibes." It is human nature to have this sense of knowing, but for Christians it is called discernment.

Sometimes Christians do not appear any different from an unsaved person if we see them through our eyes. (Let the obvious be revealed. Many have not matured spiritually.) God, the Spiritual being, will tell you something different; "She's mine," or "He's one of My children." The Holy Spirit within us craves for us to be a duplicate of Jesus Christ, a perfect replica of Him. We receive the gifts God promised us, such as speaking in tongues, prophecy, wisdom, teachers, visions, dreams, and love. We have the Spirit to know how and when to fight off demons. I fight the dirty devil and his angels daily. It's normal for me because it's normal for me to be in His presence 24/7. I do not rearrange my schedule to pray for someone or make excuses to get out of doing my job as a child of our Heavenly Father. I have heard others say, "I don't feel like praying for others sometimes, but I'll do it anyways," or "It's not easy for me to pray for strangers or certain people." Does this sound like God's voice? Are we not supposed to imitate His ways in all things? The love of God is not coming from Christians when they say such nonsense. They are doing the works of God without love, which is the opposite of God's commandment to us.

"Love those as you love yourselves".
"Love those who hate you …"

God says He is looking for His children who worship Him in Spirit (not out of Spirit) and in Truth (not religious misunderstandings which interpret their own truths). God is a Spirit; therefore, you need to be in the Spirit to communicate with Him and to have a heartfelt change towards others. If you have to make yourself believe you love someone or make yourself talk to someone "less" than you, you are very wrong.

This is how "religious" people work, think, and act, but it is not God's way.

> "**If you really fulfill** the royal law according to the Scripture, 'You shall love your neighbor as yourself,' you are doing well. **But if you show partiality,** you are committing sin and are convicted by the law of transgressors."
>
> **James 2:8**

To show partiality (favor) to a person based on what you see as their self-worth is to do the work of the devil. How would you feel if someone thought that you were not worth his or her time? I am trying to get Christians out of this "stinking thinking." If you react this way towards others, you still do not know the love of the Father. To know the love of the Father is to see others as He sees them, through His eyes and not through your flesh. It is not the way we think that needs to change first, but our hearts. Once the heart beats to God's rhythm, the mind will rewire its way of thinking by growing in wisdom and knowledge of Him. As my friend Eddie used to always tell me, "Rose, I love the way you're wired!" When we gain more knowledge of who Christ is and renew our minds, our tangled wires will become straight.

> "**For as the body apart from the Spirit is dead, so also faith apart from works is dead.**"
>
> **James 2:26**

God clearly says, **"We cannot enter the kingdom of God by our works."** Jesus said He would have not told us to do something if He thought it was impossible. We make living harder when we do not know that God the Father, through Jesus Christ, has become one with us and has supplied all our spiritual weapons to live victoriously. Jesus has finished all works on the cross through His resurrection. He has rested; therefore we should not "try" to do, but simply BE!

"WHEN EVERYTHING ABOUT YOU
DIES, AND THERE IS NOTHING
LEFT BUT JESUS, EVERYTHING
FALLS INTO PLACE."

ROSEMARY V. CANTU

4

THE WALK OF A DISCIPLE

"May the God of hope fill you with all joy and
peace in believing, so that by the power of the
Holy Spirit you may abound in hope."
Romans 15:13

A Christian should walk through life free from bondage that
ties you to the world. Things that normally would have made
you feel depressed, mad, or even brought you happiness will
appear differently now. Our new expectation is to live fully
beyond our senses. Christ has given us the Comforter, the
Holy Spirit who lives in our inner self. Christian life is not
merely a state of mind or a feel-good sensation. It is living
love out loud from the heart and walking in the fullness of
the Spirit of God. *"I am the light of the world. Whoever
follows me will not walk in darkness, but will have the
light of life."* **John 8:12.** What is it like to be a Christian?

Many will say it is a struggle, then follow up with, "but I can do all things through Christ." Do not get me wrong, there are scriptures that support different opinions, but scripture can be misunderstood. Many people use the Word of God to justify their own views. Paul states in 2 Timothy 4:3,

> **"For the time is coming when people will not endure sound teaching, but having itching ears they will accumulate for themselves teachers to suit their own passions."**

Why do many believers say that being a Christian is hard work? The simple answer is because of how they live; therefore, it must be so. People teach others based on their own experiences. The answer to the question why Christianity is hard work is within the question. Christianity is viewed as *work*, but Jesus Christ said His way is for the simple. *"My yoke is easy, and my burden is light."* **(Matthew 11:30).** Jesus carried our burdens for us. At the cross, He exchanged His perfect righteousness for our sins. No, we did not receive His righteousness when Jesus took on our sins. He emptied Himself of righteousness to carry the sins of the world. Righteousness and sin cannot be together since they are opposed to one another.

**"For our sake he made him to be sin who knew
no sin, so that in him we might become the
righteousness of God."**
2 Corinthians 5:21

Righteousness comes *when Christ is accepted* by grace
through faith. Metaphorically speaking, a single drop of food
coloring added to a bowl of water will alter the entire matter.
One drop of Jesus's blood changes our entire being. Now, you
may think that He exchanged His goodness for our sins but
there's something we must do to get that exchange. When
Jesus was hanging on the cross, a man with no sin became
sin in hope that we may have life. So, when did you become
righteous in His eyes? This exchange can only happen when
a person believes in Jesus Christ as their Lord and Savior. It
is a joy to know the freedom we can live by following Christ.

**"For if while we were enemies we were
reconciled to God by the death of his Son,
much more, now that we are reconciled, shall
we be saved by his life."**
Romans 5:10

In 2009, my life changed forever. Though I became
a Christian around age 11, I was uneducated in the true
meaning of the Gospel. I would attend church, go home
with that Sunday's message, and try to live by the positive
thinking preached for the days ahead. I read the Bible, but I

never studied scripture for myself. I did not realize that there was such a thing as studying the Bible. I memorized quite a few verses, because that was the only way I knew what to do as a Christian. I thought the more I memorized verses and learned to explain Bible stories, the closer I got to God. I was living my life the best I knew how, yet I had difficulty fighting off ungodly desires. My life was a rollercoaster, and soon I hated life. I would get so angry with myself that I would yell and at times became abusive towards myself.

Later during my marriage, my husband Kevin accepted Jesus, and the Holy Spirit started revealing Himself. At this time, we lived with my parents. After work, the kids and I would get in the car with my husband and go for a long drive. These nights were our times to talk about our day, and Kevin always brought up God. Thanks be to God, Kevin was teaching me things that Christ was teaching him. At first, I did not accept the Truth. Every car ride turned into an argument. It seemed that each time the Lord taught Kevin something new, he would share it with me. I argued with him and told him he was in too deep with his new thoughts about the meaning of the cross. Since I was not taught from God's standpoint, this new teaching was foreign to me. I will never forget when I told Kevin, "There is no way Jesus can love us that much!" I went as far as contemplating divorce because I thought he had become part of a cult. Weeks later, my heart was aching to find the truth. (I later realized it was the Holy Spirit drawing me to Himself!) At this time,

I was not working, which gave me a lot of alone time at home. Every day I immersed myself in the Bible, while Kevin continued to tell me more about Jesus. No matter the hour of the day, I could not get enough of God's Word. Within a few days, the veil lifted from my eyes, and my spirit was renewed immediately! God blessed me with spiritual gifts instantly. Ever since, my life has no longer been a rollercoaster and I live in freedom knowing my life's worth in God's eyes.

> **"For this commandment that I command you today is not too hard for you, neither is it far off. It is not in heaven, that you should say, 'Who will ascend to heaven for us and bring it to us, that we may hear it and do it? Neither is it beyond the sea, that you should say, 'Who will go over the sea for us and bring it to us, that we may hear it and do it?' But the word is very near you. It is in your mouth and in your heart, so that you <u>can</u> do it."**
>
> **Deut. 30: 11-14**

God always remembers what He has spoken, which is why He repeats it in the New Testament.

⌒◯

> **"But the righteousness based on faith says, 'Do not say in your heart, 'Who will ascend into heaven?'" (that is, to bring Christ down), or**

> 'Who will descend into the abyss?'" (that is, to
> bring Christ up from the dead). But what does
> it say? "The word is near you, in your mouth
> and in your heart …"
>
> **Romans 10:6-8**

Now that you have the Spirit of Christ in your heart by acceptance through faith, Godly living is living with a clear vision of purpose, knowledge and blessings. A "Christian" living from the flesh and not in the spirit is no different from an unsaved person living from the flesh. They carry the same thoughts as an unbeliever and are merely labelling themselves as Christians. If living freely means blending in with others and **a lack of conviction**, I would question if there was true salvation. This may offend some, but God's word is easy. A simple answer to life is yes or no; black or white.

Some of God's children overexert themselves because they work from a religious platform. "I pray and pray but nothing happens." A very popular saying is, "I try to be this best person I can be." This type of attitude comes from someone who lacks understanding. No need to worry because the spirit inside your heart is softly whispering, "You're better than this. Focus on me and my light of righteousness." (A paraphrase of the many ways our Heavenly Father speaks to his children.)

**"Take my yoke upon you, and learn from me,
for I am gentle and lowly in heart, and you will
find rest for your souls."**
Matthew 11:29

When I worked for a church ministry, people were always gossiping. Someone was always promoting themself above another church member or unbelievers. It really bothered me to work around such drivel. A popular saying from the church is, "We need to keep our friends close and our enemies closer." Wow! This could not be further from the truth. These conversations come from those who do not understand the love of God or the understanding of His will.

**"Let each of us please his neighbor for his
good, to build him up."**
Romans 15:2

Have you been in a situation when a nonbeliever put you in a corner leaving you speechless? If an unbeliever is gaining ground on you, it is because you are unprepared for the battle. You have not come to the knowledge of God's Word. He has already given us every weapon we need to be a soldier for God. As Christians, we have the power to love them unconditionally and stand still on the battleground. We have the power to fight and stop the arrows of darkness coming our way with the shield of faith. The unbelievers are without knowledge, not knowing they walk in the dark realms of this world. You are saved, and God expects more from you. How can an unbeliever come to know Christ the proper way when we share their same negative emotions? And why would they want to convert to Christ when seeing believers destroy each other will only make them think twice about needing God? Deep in our soul, God gives the power to reveal truth to all mankind. That is why sometimes an unbeliever will recognize our flaws or say something behind our backs like, "Wow! Church going people sure know how to party!" Those are powerful punches, but they are right to say them. We are to be the light of this world. Wherever we are, Christians are being watched and are expected to live differently. We are to agree and say what God says.

Doubt: "I don't have much, but at least I have God."
Faith: "Oh, fear the Lord, you his saints, for those who fear Him have <u>no</u> lack!" Psalm 34:9

What part of this verse is hard to understand? You are not growing spiritually as a Christian if you are always believing lies. We are taking on the language of the world and yet trying to justify the rough roads of life. Scripture says, "The devil also believes in God and trembles." Something must take place for us to stand out for Christ. There are a few who speak this way because they are still infants in Christ. Even a preacher can only preach milk if he has not fully matured in the Lord. You cannot hear good preaching if you do not hear the voice of God. Paul addresses infant followers of Christ in this manner:

> **"But I, brothers, could not address you as spiritual people, but as people of the flesh, as infants in Christ. I fed you with milk, not solid food, for you were not ready for it. And even now you are not yet ready, for you are still of the flesh."**
>
> **1 Corinthians 3:1-3**

Another issue that Christians believe is that they have full control of everything in their life; therefore, we do not have to suffer since all we need to say is, "I don't have to allow anything I don't want to happen in my life because I am a child of God." Well, not exactly. We were never promised a carefree life. In fact, Jesus tells us that we *will* have tribulation in this world (John 16:33) and will suffer trials (James 1:2). Do Christians have full control of everything? Only in the spiritual realm, and *ONLY* if you are walking in the Spirit, not just proclaiming that you are. It is living from the Spirit through faith and being led by the Spirit. Trials in life were not excluded from God's plan for our Christian walk. If someone is not experiencing persecution, trials, or problems, they should question if they are really living for Christ. Anyone going against the grain will <u>always</u> encounter challenges. (As far as persecution, churches use this word to describe situations in which they are hated. Until you have been physically attacked or confronted with severe threats of harassment because of your Christian lifestyle, then you cannot claim to have been persecuted, since this is the meaning behind the word.)

Are we conquerors in Christ? Yes! So, do we experience trials? Of course! That is why God called us conquerors in Christ. In order for us to become conquerors, we must be in a situation to conquer. The battles that we conquer (for those who stand in faith) are our trials and tribulations. God says in Ephesians 6:12,

> **"Put on the whole armor of God, that you *may be able* to stand against the schemes of the devil. For we do not wrestle against flesh and blood, but against the rulers, against the authorities, against the cosmic powers over this present darkness, against the spiritual forces of evil in the heavenly places."**

This speaks of spiritual warfare. What does God mean when he says, *'that you may be able'*? Please do not misinterpret this scripture. It does not mean we *may* lose some and *may* win some. This battle requires you to fight in faith and by faith which determines your outcome. God does not promise *us* a successful victory, but a successful victory *is* promised. In other words, when you are fighting a spiritual battle and decide to give up or recognize defeat, Satan still loses because of Jesus. He may ask you to lay down your life for the Gospel, but you will always be the one who truly conquered. You are still one of God's children, which makes you a warrior for the winning team. A victory is won when we are clothed in Him in faith and wear our armor of God. Amen!

Let's take an example of Ryan at work. He has been going through a trial against those who oppose his belief. Ryan is unwavering in standing firm on God's Word, ready to be fired or reprimanded at work for the gospel of Christ. He is finally let go, but then God blesses him with a better job, more pay, better hours, etc. Standing by God's Word may contradict their rules about religion in the workplace. I have experienced this firsthand more than once and God has always stood up for me. You may have heard of believers around the United States who have been sued for not retreating from their faith. These trials are viewed publicly on television, which is a huge testimony for Christ.

In 2016, I went to work not expecting confrontation so early in the morning. In my classroom, on the inside of my door was a poster of a cartoon character waving hi. I decided to write "Have a blessed day!" next to the character's paw. One early morning, I received an email from my boss to take down the poster because it offended someone. She asked me to go to her office to meet with her. At the end of the day, I made my way to see her. She politely explained to me that she was a religious person just like me, but she needed to keep God out of the school. I felt inspired by the Spirit to defend the Lord. Filled with the Spirit, I told her that I was not a religious person, but that I am a Christian who is a child of God and that there was nothing wrong with the word *blessed*. With a gentle smile, I told her that I would not take down the poster, but that she was welcome to do so herself if it offended her. Immediately, I saw that I was not dealing with her but with an evil spirit who was testing me. The spirit manifested himself through her. The room became dark in the spiritual realm. It was as if the room disappeared. She drew herself close to me, leaving just inches between us. Her eyes literally became blood red, as did her face as she yelled, asking if I was refusing to take down the poster. Calmly, I said yes. She quickly grabbed her bag and left the office. The next morning, I was written up for insubordination. Two weeks later, as I was walking past her office, she called me in to visit with her. She laughed as she explained that she had just received an email from the Superintendent, which he ended with, "Have a blessed day." She explained to me that she was doing her job by keeping God out and that "blessed" was unacceptable, but now she was confused. Although she did not retract the write-up to my knowledge, she knew she did wrong. I glorified God and cried to Him with a thankful heart when I returned to my room. I conquered the trial that the devil thought he was sure to win!

Another incident (for there are many) occurred in 2013. I was working at a high school for a department specializing with Academic Programs. I was temporarily helping for a few weeks until the secretary returned from maternity leave.

During my second day, an Assistant Principal came into the office to visit with an employee. Noticing me on his way out of the office, he introduced himself. "Albert" was very friendly and made easy conversation by asking me questions about myself. I told him I was a minister for Christ. I explained the reason I decided to leave my previous position and work as a substitute. (It was because of the ability to set my schedule, giving me time for the ministry.) As he became interested in our topic of conversation, he asked if I could pray for his grandson. I obviously had to free him from his bondage, so I shared with him the love and power of God, and that he could pray for his grandson, too. Every word I spoke, he cherished in his heart. As we continued to speak every day, I learned that he was hungry to know more about Jesus. That was exciting to know!

A few weeks later, I was asked to assist in the front office. As I prepared to work the front desk, Albert greeted me good morning and asked if I could visit him in his office. Once again, he was very interested in the God I served. We spoke for a little while, and I answered questions he had about my faith. As I was heading back to my desk, I saw a student on crutches, and since he was standing next to my desk, I asked what happened to his right calf muscle. He looked at me with confusion, but also with excitement. He asked, "How did you know that?" I proceeded to tell him about God. I asked him to stand on his hurt leg because the pain had left. As he stood, he quickly started to jump on the leg, as if he were trying to jump-start himself. I could not help but laugh. This kid was in awe of the miracle Jesus Christ had just performed. He gave me a hug and left the office, but not before he told others what had just happened. (He reminded me of the same excitement when Jesus healed the blind man by the Bethsaida pool. He also went about telling everyone around him what happened.) Later that day, Albert asked me if I had prayed for a student on crutches. I boldly told him yes. He said that the student was a member of the Student Council and an honor student. The student had stopped by to see him and told him of what happened to his leg. Albert expressed the excitement the boy was experiencing. He started speaking to me about the wonderful works of God needed in his school.

But one of the best experiences I had besides spreading the gospel and seeing people healed was the day Albert pulled me away from my work and into his office once again. There, sitting quietly and upset, was a boy slouching in a chair. Albert introduced us and told the student that I walk in the power of God, and that he invited me to talk to him (where the counselors had failed). I quickly recognized the excitement in Albert's eyes and smiled. Sitting in his rolling chair, he pushed himself out of the way, as if he expected a spectacle. I veered to look at him a final time before focusing on the student. I grinned at Albert as he relaxed in his chair, resting his chin on his fist as he waited with anticipation. I redirected my attention to the boy slouched carelessly in his chair. I remember looking at him for a while, then I asked him why he was making the choice to live a hard life (although I knew the reason). As he shrugged his shoulders, I told him that I knew he was feeling sick, and his head was hurting a lot. I asked him, "Can I prove that Jesus is real and that he loves you?" As he nodded yes, I commanded the headache and heaviness in him to leave. I told him to go drink some water and that by the time he comes back in all his pain would be gone. Obediently, he left. While he was gone, Albert asked me how I knew he had a headache. I replied by saying that Jesus is real. When the student returned, I asked, "Ok, it's done. How do you feel?" He sat up straight with a slight smile on his face and said his headache and pains were gone. Full of excitement to witness the power of God, Albert kept asking the student if it was really gone. Albert was so ecstatic that he was pushing the student to believe in God!

It's amazing how God moves whenever we live in His presence. Albert bypassing the counselors' office and asking me to help the student was the work of God. I know of people who preach based on their experiences as a believer but do not fully understand how to walk in the Spirit. Talking to others about how to walk in Christ or how to walk in his gifts does not mean that someone has truly accepted Christ's gifts themselves. But if you live in the Spiritual Realm, you can quickly discern a preacher or teacher's position. Unfortunately, many pastors limit God. They know a lot about God, but discerning the truth depends on you. As

Believers, we should be taught by the Holy Spirit and not by humans. Is it wrong to listen to preachers, teachers, or evangelists? Absolutely not! But if you do not die to who you are, or if you do not live in a continuous relationship with the Father, then how can you be teachable and able to discern Truth? God says, "My children hear My voice." I constantly hear Him speak to me daily, and you can too. The Lord and I laugh together, I converse with Him, and God has never left me hanging with a question. Revelation is easy to come by, but we must die in our flesh and not follow every doctrine out there.

"For whatever was written in former days was written for our instruction, that through endurance and through the encouragement of the Scriptures (not man) we might have hope."
Romans 15:4

It has become normal for churches to teach based on their own experiences. It is very important to live from your spirit so that God can reveal truth to you.

Let me share this with you. The devil works through people. God works through people. They both need a physical body in which to dwell. The difference between the two is that Jesus Christ requires your permission to be inside you. To whom would you rather give license to? The Father of

Destruction, or the Father of Salvation? Who is the one that makes you feel dirty and gives you the urge to turn to drugs, sex, to drinking, rebelliousness, and to feel hate for others who "deserve it"? The devil comes to kill, steal, and destroy. He will kill your body with diseases, drugs, suicide, murder, or other crimes. He will steal your joy, hope, health, money, peace, and everything good in your life. And the devil will destroy your mind with lies and thoughts of destruction. Satan will destroy your marriage and your relationship with your family and will make you question your relationship with God. Wouldn't you rather give your heart to the one who gives peace, love, self-worth, hope, a forgiving heart for others and unimaginable blessings?

"TO BE ACCEPTED BY ALL, IS A
PATH FOR DISAPPOINTMENT."

ROSEMARY V. CANTU

5

@

THE SWORD OF THE SPIRIT

"If we live by the Spirit, let us also keep in step with the Spirit."

Galatians 5:25

When you have been baptized by the Holy Spirit, you experience a new beginning within yourself. Another new door will soon open, like the one that opened when you accepted Jesus Christ. **"I stand at the door and knock. If anyone hears my voice and opens the door, I will come in to him and eat with him, and he with me." Rev.3:20.** You now have the fullness of God the Father and the Holy Spirit working and living inside. The problem most Christians have is thinking that God will control us like puppets on strings since "He's in control." Is He really in full control?

After my first year of marriage, I was so eager to become a mom. During that time, it did not take me long to realize that

Kevin and I grew up very differently. I grew up in a religious home, but his lifestyle told a different story. We realized our different upbringings might create conflict between us as parents. I told Kevin there had to be balance in how we raise our children. Coming from a strict home, I had to learn leniency, while Kevin had to learn how to be strict. I knew exactly how I was going to love and raise my children.

In 1999, we had our first child, Katelyn. I wanted to teach her independence to become a strong leader and think for herself, to be courageous, never give up, to obey instructions and to love everyone. With these traits embedded firmly in her heart, I could trust her to do what was right as she grew. We also had a son, Zachary, three years later. He grew up strong in these traits as well. As much as I love them, I had to let them make their own decisions. In many areas we guided them through life by offering different solutions to their problems so they could learn to think outside the box. Kevin and I didn't 'make' them do something simply because we were their parents; instead we taught them family values and morals to live by.

Our Heavenly Father works the same way. Starting way back in Genesis, Adam and Eve were not controlled by God. He blessed them because they were His. God said to them,

"Be fruitful and multiply and fill the earth and subdue it and have dominion over the fish of the sea and over the birds of the heavens and over every living thing that moves on the

earth." And God said, "Behold, I have given you every plant yielding seed that is on the face of all the earth, and every tree with seed in its fruit. You shall have them for food. And to every beast of the earth and to every bird of the heavens and to everything that creeps on the earth, everything that has the breath of life, I have given every green plant for food."

Genesis 1:28-30

God visited them daily, always keeping His eye on them. **"And they heard the sound of the Lord God walking in the garden in the cool of the day." (Gen 3:8).** Adam and Eve did not ask God to guide them or beg Him to stay. That is something the Lord enjoyed and did willingly. Every morning when I wake up, I do not focus on myself. My thoughts automatically focus on my children. Our Lord works the same way, but even better. You have a God who never sleeps, so you are always on His mind.

How did the fall of man change the course for every generation?

And the Lord commanded the man saying, "You may surely eat of every tree of the garden, but of the tree of the knowledge of good and evil you shall not eat, for in the day that you eat of it you shall surely die."

Gen 2:16-17

Eve made the ultimate decision on her own to disobey God's command. She had two choices: obey the voice of the Lord or listen to the voice of another. Did God withdraw Himself from them? No, they created division between themselves and God. Holiness and sin cannot exist together. Immediately, a veil covered their eyes, the curtain was brought down, and darkness was in motion on the earth. (When Jesus died on the cross, the curtain was torn, no longer separating Law and God. The veil was lifted when you receive Christ and Jesus conquered darkness when He rose from the grave.) Eating of the fruit ultimately led to years of turmoil. Later on, people relied on the Laws and Prophets to bring them teachings and warnings from God. He never abandoned them and always reached out to the lost. It was up to them to either follow His commands or face their own consequences. God is not in control of your life but allows you to choose for yourselves.

God told Abraham that he was going to bless Sarah with a son. God spoke to each of them separately, informing them that they were going to be blessed with a child. Sarah, running low on patience after lack of conceiving, told Abraham to lay with another woman. Abraham became uneasy from the pressure of Sarah's words, yet did as she asked of him. Abraham then laid with Sarah's servant, Hagar and conceived a son. Though God promised them a child, they wanted it on their time. Disobeying God, Hagar's son,

Ishmael and his offspring brought suffering and fighting amongst the people.

People will always have the free will to choose to please themselves or to please God. God is a gentleman and will never force His will on you. If that were the case, ALL Christians would be living the perfect life in the flesh and Spirit. It is very possible to live like Christ, and we can make the choice to live a spiritual life. The ultimate decision is up to you.

As children of God, we have the Holy Spirit within us. Holy means pure, righteous and without blemish. When you immerse yourself in God's Spirit, you allow Him to dwell, guide, and correct you. When I say to immerse yourself, that does not mean that you alone have the power to fill yourself with the Holy Spirit. To be fully empowered by God's Spirit, you must no longer live your life for you. Because of your renewed spirit, you gladly become a living sacrifice for God. This is what it means to be in a commutative relationship with the Spirit of God. The question now is, what is the Sword of the Spirit? Yes, the Word of God. The difference is between the way you were versus living faithfully in the Holy Spirit.

When you have become a living sacrifice and live for His purpose only, the Holy Spirit can speak to you personally and through you. The possibilities of Spiritual knowledge are endless! You have open communication with God and

Jesus our Lord. Your spiritual senses are activated to receive messages from the throne of God.

One afternoon as I was on my way to pick up my kids from school, I sneezed. No one was in the car with me, so I made a little self-pitying remark, "Aww, no one is here to tell me 'God bless you.'" (Yes, I often speak to myself, lol.) Instantly, God spoke to me and said, "*I* bless you." He said it with a funny tone, and I laughed for quite some time. When God said He would never leave nor forsake you, He meant it! He is always ready to communicate, so be ready to listen.

I used to think that Jesus would never talk to someone like me— that God had more important people to talk to. This was a lie from Satan, as I later learned by growing into my identity in Christ. As a Christian, I never had an open line of communication with Jesus. I did not know it existed. I thought God spoke to Moses and the prophets just to get us where we are now. Fortunately, God is the same yesterday, today, and tomorrow and His word never changes. As I mentioned previously, my heart melted to know the depths of God's heart. This is what allowed me to hear the Spirit of God and have conversations with Christ. When you come to understand His love for you, your heart feels the urge to know Him deeper. It is more than reading some verses. The love for truth compels you to dissect scripture and to go beyond your own narrow-minded thinking. This is allowing the Spirit, who is your Helper, to guide you to His Truth.

"When the Spirit of truth comes, he will guide you into all the truth, for he will not speak on his own authority, but whatever he hears he will speak, and he will declare to you the things to come."

John 16:13

LIE
"I DON'T HAVE MUCH, BUT
AT LEAST I HAVE GOD."

TRUTH
"OH, FEAR THE LORD, YOU
HIS SAINTS, FOR THOSE WHO
FEAR HIM HAVE NO LACK!"

PSALM 34:9

6

(heart symbol)

HEAR GOD ABOVE MAN

"I will put my laws into their minds, and write them on their hearts, and I Will be their God, and they shall be my people."

Hebrews 8:10

ONE EYE

Our eyes need to be fastened on Christ Jesus, never on man. Of course people can *inspire* us, but we should not wish to be like another. God made you different to share the gospel in your own unique way. You have a divine purpose to fulfill, and no one can do your job better than you. As a minister, I can only teach you about the love of Christ. I cannot force you to understand it or make you love Him with your whole heart. Several people have told me that they wish they were bold like me. The problem is they would not be able to imitate me exactly. We were all made unique for His purpose.

Have you ever been around someone you wished you were like? Before you knew it, being around them constantly brought the two of you closer and more alike. Yet, you never will be the 'original,' but just an imitation. Love who God made *you* to be and be the best at it! From the minute you renounce your life for Christ, your heart will never be the same. A new relationship is born, and your new journey begins. It is an indescribable feeling when you receive God's revelation for your life. It becomes evident that you are a child of God. You will find yourself focusing on Him throughout the peaceful times and during challenging trials. The gospel will no longer be mere words and God's word will become alive. As you read His Word, the Spirit teaches you far beyond the written words, imparting also treasured information from His heart to yours. When you study God's Word in the Spirit, start expecting to hear from Him.

> **"I, I am the LORD, and besides me there is no savior. I declared and saved and proclaimed, when there was no strange god among you; and you are my witnesses," declares the LORD, "and I am God."**
>
> **Isaiah 43:11-12**

God is a God of love and a jealous God. He does not want to be overlooked or replaced by someone else. Paul told his followers to "imitate me." Paul did not mean to imitate his actions, nor to talk or teach like him. We should not imitate any man; our eyes need to be on Jesus. By revelation, when Paul said, "imitate me," he was referring to the way he followed the teaching of Christ, obeyed Christ, and communed spiritually with God. Remember, God never contradicts Himself. In the following scripture, He states exactly who we should follow.

"Therefore, be imitators of God, as beloved children."

Ephesians 4:1

This is how we should also be with Christ. Christ left His kingdom to be our prime example. He wants us to follow only Him, be like Him. God clearly states that we are not under a shadow. This no longer exists as it did under the old covenant.

When he said above, "You have neither desired nor taken pleasure in sacrifices and offerings and burnt offerings and sin offerings" (these are offered according to the law), then he added, "Behold, I have come to do your will." He does away with the first in order to establish the second. And by that will we have been sanctified through the offering of the body of Jesus Christ once for all."

Hebrews 10:8-10

**"He who dwells in the shelter of the Most High
will abide in the shadow of the Almighty."**
(Psalms 91:1)

Under the old covenant, only a high priest could enter the Holy of Holies, once a year. The sacrifices of bulls and goats would atone for sins, but this left man always conscious of his sins. *"For by works of the law no human being will be justified in his sight, since through the law comes knowledge of sin."* (Romans 3:20). Jesus came to fulfill the law by abolishing it. We are now under a new covenant with Christ.

> **"Therefore, brothers, since we have confidence to enter the holy places by the blood of Jesus, by the new and living way that he opened for us through the curtain, that is, through his flesh, and since we have a great priest over the house of God, let us draw near with a true heart in full assurance of faith, with our hearts sprinkled clean from an evil conscience and our bodies washed with pure water."**
> **Hebrew 10:19-22**

When we abide with our Lord Jesus Christ and focus on God, we are safe under Him. In the Old Testament, a cloud would follow God's people to show the Spirit was "upon them" and "in them." (The Spirit of God always existed from the beginning, but it was temporal.) He lives in the deepest part of our hearts now. Growing up, I remember my dad speaking words of wisdom whenever a lesson needed to be taught. Dad would always tell me, "your eyes are the windows to your heart, so always watch your mouth and the way you live your life."

Luke 11:34 says, ***"Your eye is the lamp of your body."*** It does not say your <u>eyes are</u> a lamp of your body. Why did God refer the eye in a singular noun? His plan for us was not to have double vision or look around at our surroundings. The Lord repeatedly says to focus AHEAD in the direction of God our Father.

Many teachings express the importance of a Christians position needing to be sharpened. Examples such as, we should always be aware of our surroundings; sheep among wolves should be aware of all the "what if's"; we should worry about our reputations and how others perceive us. These careless thoughts can keep us from our freedom in Christ. In a teaching I listened to years ago, we were taught to be ready when we get attacked by the enemy. But to be ready, we should study how the devil works, how diseases may be caused (due to certain sins), and so on. Learning all the 'but's' and 'how's' as to why we should study the enemy's schemes and evil works only draws us away from God's truth and from directing our attention on Him. Studying evil spirits will only get you caught up in the dark realm. The author of the Bible (God) never said to study our surroundings or live according to other perspectives. God says to focus on Him! He has already written about the kind of world we live in, the weapons the devil will use and his deceitful devices against

Christians. Why do we need to be taught the how's, when's, where's and why's? Our Savior has redeemed us from this curse so that we are now conquerors for Christ. We are not overcome by this world since Jesus has overcome it already, giving us the power to defeat evil.

> **"For everyone who has been born of God overcomes the world. And this is the victory that has overcome the world—our faith. Who is it that overcomes the world except the one who believes that Jesus is the Son of God?"**
> **Hebrews 5:4-5**

As I wrote this study, the Lord gave me a vision of a sniper preparing to fire his weapon. (God works through us in a way we as individuals can understand Him.) These trained snipers position themselves to be ready and put all their focus on one subject, their target. When a sniper aims, he closes one eye to shut-out the view around him, leaving one eye open to look straight ahead into the scope. His mind is completely clear of thought, with nothing to distract his imagination. It is almost as if he is in shut-down mode. No distractions interfere with his concentration, only his focus at hand, and his target to shoot.

Our eye (one direction of focus) is the lamp of our body. Our body will radiate the Light of He who dwells in us when we live unto Him and not for ourselves. **"The light shines in the darkness, and the darkness has not overcome it."**

(**John 1:5**). When our heart desires to turn our eye towards our target Jesus Christ, then our spirit shares in Christ and defeats the devil at his own game. If our mind (spiritual thinking: "we have the mind of Christ") rests on God's promises, we will imitate Him in life.

> **"Therefore, my beloved, as you have always obeyed, so now, not only as in my presence but much more in my absence, work out your own salvation with fear and trembling, for it is God who works in you, both to will and to work for his good pleasure."**
>
> **Philippians 2: 12-13**

ONE MIND

As individuals, we all think and view issues differently and we all have our set ways of thinking. But does this apply to Christian thinking? A common misconception is that it is OK for Christians to not always see eye-to-eye as long as we serve the One True God. This is one of many lies the devil has used to deceive God's people. Is it our different views which makes each one of us unique? Statements like this one only apply to human thinking when we voice our opinions on various subject matters. For example, I may say that it is a terrible idea for a city to build a Wal-Mart near expensive subdivisions. My opinion is it will cause traffic and crime in our neighborhoods, and the market value of the surrounding homes could decrease. Yet, another person may think it will be better for the shoppers to have a store nearby, and that it may even bring more business to this part of town. Having different opinions on an issue like this probably does not matter because it does not affect our spiritual growth. However, our ideas about our spiritual walk should be alike, and it matters severely if they are different. God's law which is written on our heart of flesh, applies to all His children.

> **"So if there is any encouragement in Christ, any comfort from love, any participation in the Spirit, any affection and sympathy, complete my joy by being of the <u>same mind</u>, have the <u>same love</u>, being <u>in full accord and of one mind</u>."**
>
> **Phil. 2:1-2**

Non-believers are blinded by lies. They wear a disguise every day of their lives thinking that it is the normal way to live. I compare this kind of life to the zombies in the TV series *The Walking Dead.* These lost souls are alive, but they are not living. Sadly, people all around you are alive but not living a genuine lifestyle for Christ. If you were to tell them they have a special place in the heart of God, they probably would not believe you, or they may agree and shrug off the idea. Tell them, "God is willing to provide peace, love and forgiveness for you," and they may call you a fool.

Are you wearing a mask? Do you have a large beam in one eye? Are you judging people by whether they are saved or not, or by who bears more spiritual fruit than another? In my experience, a Christian who makes a point to constantly correct other Christians is holding on to a lot of jealousy. Using the whip on others to correct them is a simple game of persuasion and self-satisfaction, or better said by God, it is a game of *self-righteousness*. If a jealous person can control the dress code or fix the "problem" of someone else, then they now have one less person to be threatened by. A person behaving this way has become legalistic by following a law made for the purpose of self-gratification. This mind set is far from God's way of thinking. If this was God's way to fix one another, then Christians would be pointing fingers at each other and causing a world of chaos and emotional scars.

In John 8, the Pharisees bring to Jesus a woman who had committed adultery. Jesus says that anyone who was without sin was able to cast the first stone. One by one, they leave empty-handed, leaving Jesus alone with the women. Jesus tells her that he does not condemn her, but to sin no more. There are three powerful lessons within this setting. First, Jesus did not point out to her what she was doing was wrong. Confronted by Love, she knew in her heart that her actions were sinful, and she felt ashamed. Secondly, He did not lecture her or try to change her ways. Jesus said He did not condemn her or judge her. Finally, Jesus did not worry about what others would think of Him being alone with a woman, especially an adulteress. He never acted or reacted according to other people's views. His heart is always righteous, and that is all that counts. Your heart tells the true meaning of your intentions, regardless of others' opinions. This is why Jesus will judge the hearts of men.

There are multiple viewpoints pertaining to scripture but why do Christians think differently? It's most likely they have their own religious beliefs and that seems to be more accurate than God's Word. They do not understand the truth of the Lord's Grace. God rescued the lost sheep because they were wandering off cluelessly, right? Christ has become our perfect Shepherd to teach us all things. On the day of your salvation, you have been saved from wandering blind.

> **"But when one turns to the Lord, the veil is removed. Now the Lord is the Spirit, and where the Spirit is, there is FREEDOM."**
> **2 Corinthians. 3:17**

This is one of my favorite verses: *"...where the Spirit is, there IS freedom."* 2 Corinthians 3:17. But freedom from what? The answer is straightforward: freedom from being trapped as you. You were never meant to live in this world through the flesh, but in freedom as God intended you and I to live, which is through Jesus Christ our Lord. Jesus saved you by bringing you home under His wings, under His protection, under His peace and rest as His child. Now that you have accepted this truth, you do not have the right to live freely according to your own mind. Christians were never told, "Now let your minds wander, but live in the Spirit." Living lukewarm is not His intention for us.

When a person undergoes psychological counseling, the experience can often be destructive instead of beneficial. For example, Victor has just lost his wife in a tragic accident. He confesses that he is burdened by guilt, sorrow, anger, and depression. His psychiatrist completes a psychological evaluation, writes a prescription, and then concludes Victor is unstable and is showing Bipolar symptoms. Believing there is something very wrong with him, he is medicated and suicidal because of an incorrect opinion.

The same concept applies to God's chosen people. You may have been told you are still a sinner because you are only human. Unfortunately, everyone has experienced having this disturbing conversation at some point and it's such a shame to hear it from believers. God's children have been told this lie for many, many years. The danger is that after hearing so many watered-down sermons, you may start to believe it. Sin is now accepted in the lives of God's people. You are now in danger from the lost world by living their ways, yet still labeling yourself a Christian. Whether you feel guilty for committing a sin or not, subconsciously you remember that you "are only human." You have stunted your growth as a newly created being, hurting your walk with Christ by living a lie. How can the world witness true imitators of

Christ among them if we live just like the others? Our minds need to be renewed.

> **"But that is not the way you learned Christ!- assuming that you have heard about him and were taught in him, as the truth is in Jesus, to put off your old self, which belongs to your former manner of life and is corrupt through deceitful desires, and to be renewed in the spirit of your mind, and to put on the new self, created after the likeness of God in true righteousness and holiness."**
>
> **Eph.4:20-24**

Wandering minds are dangerous and destructive to themselves and to others. The Father says to think of love and things that are pure and righteous. It is easy to live through the Father in Jesus Christ, but it is hard to live up to the person you think you should be. If Christian life is a challenge for you, I will bet that you are straddling the fence with one foot in and one foot out, living a lukewarm life. Your new life must be played with a full deck of hearts. As I often say, "It's a heart thing!" Life in Christ is not a struggle, but a simple free way of living! Amen.

"I CAN BECAUSE HE HAS!"

ROSEMARY V CANTU

7

SPIRIT REVEALED

"The brothers immediately sent Paul and Silas
away to Barea, and when they arrived they went
into the Jewish synagogues. Now these Jews
were more noble than those in Thessalonica;
they received the word with all eagerness,
examining the Scriptures daily to see if these
things were so. Many of them believed."

Acts 17:10-11

Reading these verses, my heart became like butter on a hot
skillet. At that moment, I saw God in His endless ways. God
wrote the perfect book to answer all our questions so there is
no doubt or confusion. Unlike many people today, the Jews
did not take to heart what Paul and Silas were preaching.
Even though they were apostles of Christ, the Jews did not

just accept what Paul and Silas said but instead went home and *searched scripture for themselves*!

Some Christians enjoy fellowship with each other outside of church, which is acceptable. Many people attend church, Bible college, or conferences to broaden their knowledge. Regardless of where you receive the gospel, it is important to discern truth. Many are too open-minded and take in every word they hear. Then they become set in their beliefs and share their "gospel," repeating those "words of truth" to others. It is no surprise when I hear, "Well, so-and-so said all things come from God, good and bad," or "Brother Joe teaches that we should …." If you are not living from the Spirit of Truth, then how can you know what Truth is?

It is OK to listen to a teaching, but people are missing the point. If what you hear is taught by and from the Spirit, then and only then has Truth been spoken. All Truth comes from God. What if I told you to invest in GMC stock and that it would be worth $2.2 million five years from now? Would you take my word for it and invest thousands, or would you research the stock markets? A man's word must be based on the evidence of truth. Man should not be exalted as if he gave himself knowledge to teach. I know too many Christian teachers, preachers, and speakers that often mix their own opinions with scripture. It sounds scriptural, but do they back up what is written in the Bible? It comes across as fact but they are seen from one's perspective, therefore teaching what they know. We have allowed ourselves to be misled simply because the opinion was more convincing to the hearer.

Here is a perfect example. In my younger years as a Christian, I was taught that sometimes God allows bad things to happen to us. I have been told that we are not higher than the Apostle Paul, so if God did not remove the thorn from Paul's side, then we should praise God regardless of the thorn he has given to us. Almost 20 years later, I read up on the thorn of Paul and it said nothing about God giving it to him. In fact, the scriptures clearly says that the thorn Paul was referring to was to his physical attacks.

> "...with far greater labors, far more imprisonments, with countless beatings, and often near death. Five times I received at the hands of the Jews the forty lashes less one. Three times I was beaten with rods. Once I was stoned. Three times I was shipwrecked; a night and a day I was adrift at sea; on frequent journeys, in danger from rivers, danger from robbers, danger from my own people, danger from Gentiles, danger in the city, danger in the wilderness, danger at sea, danger from false brothers; in toil and hardship, through many a sleepless night, in hunger and thirst, often without food, in cold and exposure."
>
> **2 Cor. 11:23-27**

And

"So to keep me from becoming conceited because of the surpassing greatness of the revelations, a thorn was given me in the flesh (not spiritual but everything mentioned above), a messenger of Satan to harass me (the thorn was not given to Paul by God), to keep me from becoming conceited (having favor from God). Three times I pleaded with the Lord about this, that it should leave me. But he said to me, 'My grace is sufficient for you, for my power is made perfect in weakness.' Therefore, I will boast all the more gladly of my weaknesses, so that the power of Christ may rest upon me."

Satan was the one putting Paul through these trials. Contrary to the teachings, the scripture does not mention God refusing to remove the thorn.

My grace is sufficient for thee – He will not be permitted to fail under these afflictions, and his enemies will not be able to prevail against him. (Spiritual living)

My strength is made perfect in weakness – The more violently Paul is afflicted and tried, the more His power will be seen and acknowledged. In other words, a person who is persecuted for Christ, and lives to testify gives glory to God. People can only proclaim that God strengthens His people.

I will boast all the more gladly of my weaknesses – The more trials he endures, and God's grace sees him through, the more glory God receives.

Let us use the movie *Gladiator* as an analogy to explain the nature of Paul's thorn.

In this movie, Maximus, an army leader, endures the death of his wife and son. His entire army then turns their back on him. He is beaten, imprisoned, enslaved, and forced to fight and kill for the entertainment and pleasure of others. At the end, Maximus fights the ruler who has been behind all the hateful schemes. Maximus defeats the ruler and wins the love and respect of the crowd. Let us view this in a spiritual setting. Maximus is like someone highly favored by God whom Satan attacks physically and emotionally, but not spiritually. He continues to stand firm in his faith. God's grace is enough to overcome hardships and show that his spirit is unbreakable with the power of God. At the end of the movie, Maximus stands firm in the power of God, fulfills his life pleasing according to God's will, and leaves an example of a Christian for Christ.

God is ready to give understanding of His word for those who seek to find truth.

"The simple believes everything, but the prudent gives thought to his steps."

Proverbs 14:15

Did God want us to take His words "be the light" seriously? Yes, of course. Let's say you have friends with whom you drink, smoke, bad mouth, watch R-rated movies, and engage in sexual relationships. You and your friends live this way simply because you do not know Jesus as your personal Savior. There should always be a clear distinction between God's children versus the children of the devil (as Jesus puts it). Christ should be as important to you as the air you breathe. To stay alive, all you need to do is naturally breathe without thinking twice about it. The only time you think about needing air is when you find yourself short of breath and you suddenly realize you need help. Sadly, Jesus has been put in the same category. You only think of Him of when you have nowhere else to turn. Living this way is normal for many, and they do not feel guilty. If you are still doing the same things after receiving Christ, something is very wrong. You need to examine your heart and ask yourself if you sincerely became born again. Another reason may be you left your first love. Jesus also says many will stray away from the gospel.

Jesus says, "Simon, Simon, behold, Satan demanded to have you, that he might sift you like wheat, but I have prayed for you that your

faith may not fail. And when you _have turned_ _again_, strengthen your brothers."

Luke 22: 31-32

This is done so you will come to a point in your life to run back to Christ. This type of life does not represent Jesus at all. Handing someone over to destruction is a disciplinary measure to bring about repentance and a return to true discipleship, instead of being a stumbling block to other infant Christians and a false witness to non-believers. Now, ask yourself if you are a Christian who has stopped growing in Christ. If so, it is never too late to get your heart right with Jesus, who loves you very much. His arms were spread wide open for you on the cross. Now, He can wrap those same arms around you if you only believe.

> **"Keep hold of instruction; do not let go; guard her, for she is your life. Do not enter the path of the wicked, and do not walk in the way of the evil. Avoid it; do not go on it; turn away from it and pass on.**
>
> **For they cannot sleep unless they have done wrong; they are robbed of sleep unless they have made someone stumble."**
>
> **Proverbs 4:13-16**

Jesus was far from popular when He walked on earth, so why should you feel the need to be recognized by others? He was a laughingstock, mocked by everyone. Why should you need to feel untouchable? Our identity is in Jesus Christ, not our flesh. Our bodies will burn, but the light of God radiates His light within us, giving us ever-lasting life in the Spirit.

One night in 2011, I was lying in bed talking to God, and I slowly drifted off to sleep. Around 3:00 in the morning, the Lord woke me up and guided me to read Mark 13. As I read this chapter, my heart was troubled by verse 32, "But concerning that day or that hour, no one knows, not even the angels in heaven, nor the Son, but only the Father." This verse kept me from reading any further. I read it over and over many times until I finally stopped to ask God why Jesus does not know of His own coming. Immediately, He answered me, "If Jesus knew of His coming, then you would know, too." Wow! That hit me like a ton of bricks. Since we have the mind of Christ, we share in His thoughts. Scripture states that we have the mind and nature of Christ.

I am a living testimony that Christ Jesus is so awesome! He opened my eyes to understand Him deeper on a personal level. We all grow in Christ each day. The key is to grow and never give up hope. Do not sell yourself short. The Word says we have the nature of Christ. Does Christ go around saying, "I'm no good," "I'll never achieve my goals in life," "No one loves me," or "I'm always sick, or unappreciated"? No! We have everything we need to succeed in life. *For we are more than conquerors in Christ.* If you are not in Christ, then you are outside of Him. His will for your precious life can only be performed when you are walking with Him. Living outside of His will, you are exposed to everything Satan stands for. You are at his disposal, toyed with for his pleasure. If you are in physical pain, depressed, anxious, or just getting by, that is a hard life to live. I have heard excuses that it is hard to be a Christian as far back as I can remember. Well, if you do not follow the will of God, you will experience just how hard life can be. When things go against you, you are on your own, but Jesus is always ready to help when you call on Him. Jesus has promised to be our Comforter, our Prince of Peace, and our Savior from this world. God is our provider, our Father. Jesus did not leave His kingdom just to be beaten, spit upon, rejected by man, whipped, and nailed to a tree. He did not do this just so you will accept Him and get your ticket into heaven. Jesus wants to live in you and to dwell in you forever! If you are not living out loud, rejoicing in the mighty God you serve, then you are not living yet. Living means being active, in motion. Organisms, atoms, electrons, and germs are never sleeping. They all have a purpose for their existence. These amazing creations are in constant motion like our God. There is only one God, and He never sleeps or slumbers.

"I lift up my eyes to the hills. From where does my help come? My help comes from the Lord, who made heaven and earth.

> He will not let your foot be moved; he who
> keeps you will not slumber. Behold, he who
> keeps Israel will neither slumber or sleep."
>
> **Psalms 121:4**

Open your heart to the Father of Salvation, your creator, a gentle, loving God who wants to give you life and more in abundance. God does not play with us like pieces from a chess game. We must take responsibility as children of God, living to do His will and not the way we "think" is right. The day you accepted Jesus Christ was the last time you have the will to do as you want. Now, you are to live in His will for eternity, every day.

> **"Whoever has my commandments and keeps
> them, he it is who loves me. And he who love me
> will be loved by my Father, and I will love him
> and manifest myself to him."**
>
> **John 14:21**

> **"This is real love—not that we loved God, but
> that he loved us and sent his Son as a sacrifice
> to take away our sins."**
>
> **1 John 4:10**

Our beginning is not in our fallen state of sin. Our beginning is in the heart of a loving Father. This is the foundation of true fellowship with God.

"AS YOU RENEW YOUR MIND
TO THE WORD, BELIEVE OR
ELSE IT JUST BECOMES EMPTY
KNOWLEDGE."

ROSEMARY V CANTU

8

⊗

PUTTING OTHERS
BEFORE YOU

**"Remind them of these things, and charge them
before God not to quarrel about words, which
does no good, but only ruins the hearers."**
2 Timothy 2:14

Too often Christians spend their energy fixing other brothers
and sisters in Christ before fixing themselves. Deep down
in your heart, you know the kind of person you are, and the
effect it has on you and others. These could be positive or
negative thoughts. Do you judge others quickly? Do you put
yourself first most of the time? Are you approachable and
friendly to all, or do you pick certain people to approach?
These are just some examples of characteristics that do
not portray our Christ. This does not mean you are not a

Christian, but it does mean you are not being an example of Jesus Christ to the full potential God has in plan for you.

One day, I had a conversation with a pastor's daughter about the subject of seeing the flaws in others. I reminded her that God said, "Take the log out of your own eye before trying to take the splinter out of another person's eye." I was shocked to hear her say, "Well, we don't believe that. God is not talking to Christians." I later realized that everything she said and did reflected that false belief. She does have a big heart to help others in need and for that, God will bless.

> **"We who are strong have an obligation to bear with the failing of the weak, and not to please ourselves."**
>
> **Romans 15:1**

This does not mean to stand up for your beliefs by correcting others, but merely to be an example to others by helping them the way Jesus would. It is ruthless to put someone down then turn around and add a nice comment to soften the blow and expect them to feel good. For example, someone may say, "That skirt needs to be below the knee, but it looks pretty on you." The person being corrected will not hear anything after the negative remark. My husband (who is a Life Coach) once told me that anything positive said after "*but*" is unconsciously ignored. A negative comment at the end *or* beginning of a statement is a good way to make the hearer shut you out. Picture someone giving you a wonderful compliment, and you reply with a joyous smile and a "thank you." Your emotions may be uplifted at that moment, but then you get slapped with the errors of your ways. For instance, "You have such lovely, beautiful kids. I just don't think God approves of their wild haircuts." The only words that person focuses on are the negative judgements. This is not only ungodly, but it could also damage a person's faith if that person is searching for Christ. This displeases the Lord, yet it pleases the devil to have "filthy communications come out of the mouth." This is contrary to God's command.

God covers every aspect of how we are to live as children of Light and to be a Light in the darkness. In Romans 5:1, God talks about Christians being there for the weak and not for ourselves. This does not give you permission to correct all the things you dislike.

Jesus Christ was our prime example of how to speak to others. By reading God's word, we can see the love of Christ towards all. When a person looks for flaws in others, they reveal their low self-esteem. This often leads to jealousy, which consumes their hearts. We need to know God's love, so that what we see should not affect how we react towards others.

Most believers are taught to categorize people by whether they are Christians or not. Many judge what they see other people wear, whom they associate with, their personality, and so on. "Her wardrobe clearly shows she's not a Christian," or "He has tattoos everywhere, there's no way he knows God because He doesn't approve of that." If I had not heard these statements for myself, I would probably have a hard time believing God's children think this way. Jesus does not intend for us to see ourselves or others through our own perspective. God wants us to open our eyes to how God sees them. Sadly, religion teaches them to see how wrong others are so they can "fix" them. The Bible says, "One plants the seed (a believer sharing Jesus our Savior to others) and one waters (water of life and love poured by another believer sharing the gospel), and God is responsible for growing it (teachings done by the Spirit)." It is up to God to reveal Himself to others when Jesus lives inside of them. His nature becomes ours.

> "I planted, Apollos watered, but God gave the growth. So neither he who plants nor he who waters is anything, but only God who gives the growth. He who plants and he who waters are one, and each will receive his wages according to his labor. For we are God's fellow workers. You are God's field, God's building."
> 1 Corinthians 3:6-9

As Christ's elect, we are to be humble and full of love towards others without judging them. Our outside appearance is not what sends us to hell or heaven. Nowhere does the Word of God give importance to our flesh.

We are to prove that Jesus's nature is working in us by helping the weak. Their eyes may not be opened yet, since they have not understood their identity in Christ. It is a personal choice to enhance your identity as a child of God. When you get the drive to live for Him, change starts to take place in your heart. All human beings become precious to you because you are living through the Spirit.

> **"Therefore, let us not pass judgment on one another any longer, but rather decide never to put a stumbling block or hindrance in the way of a brother."**
> **Romans 14:13**

The first half of this statement clearly says NOT to pass Judgment. The second half of the verse says not to put a stumbling block or hindrance in a brother's way. People quote this scripture without knowing the rest of what Paul says. The verses following this explain the meaning of judgement. It is very important to read it in its proper context. I'm sure majority of us have been told that it means not to dress a certain way, so it does not cause another to sin by lusting. This could not be further from the truth. The Lord has told us not to fulfill the lust, not to desire our neighbor's wife, not to succumb to pleasures of the eye and so on, but to live in the Spirit. In doing so it automatically fulfills God's will, desiring the things of the Spirit and not of the flesh, and holds us accountable to work on our own salvation.

Romans 14 is referring to the way some view eating certain foods and esteem one day better than other days. God says, "The faith that you have, keep between you and God." (Romans 14:22). One brother may consider certain things *good* to eat and drink, while another brother may consider it good to *avoid* certain foods and drinks. Do not put a stumbling block in the way of others by judging them.

This scripture has been widely taught that putting a stumbling block is caused by gratifying one to lust. I recommend you to closely examine Romans 14 and ask the Lord to guide truth to your heart.

> **"Why do you pass judgment on you brother? Or you, why do you despise your brother? For we will all stand before the judgment seat of God; for it is written,**
> **"As I live, says the Lord, every knee shall bow to me, and every tongue shall confess to God."**

Each of us will give an account of ourselves to God. Therefore, let us not pass judgment on one another any longer, but rather decide never to be a stumbling block or hindrance in the way of a brother.

> *"I know and am persuaded in the Lord Jesus that nothing is unclean in itself, but it is*

unclean for anyone who thinks its unclean. For if your brother is grieved by what you eat, you are no longer walking in love."

Romans 14:15

AND

"Do not forsake of food, destroy the work of God. Everything is indeed clean, but is wrong for anyone to make another trouble by what he eats. It is good not to eat meat or drink wine or do anything (referring to verses 5-9) *that causes your brother to stumble. The faith that you have, keep between yourself and God."*

Romans 14: 20-22

We are not meant to add whatever we think this verse may possibly mean. We cannot change its meaning by saying it includes other issues in life. God did not write one verse but an entire chapter on the topic. Food, glorious food!

The Lord is the perfect author, so He knows how to write scripture. Every word in every chapter explains in detail what is being painted for the reader. When you read God's Truth filled with Spirit, so shall you be also; therefore the two, the Holy Spirit and you, are one. You are now in a position of spiritual worship to be taught by the Lord.

The Lord's children are to walk according to the Spirit every day. When a guy lusts after a female, he is responsible for his own heart. It is not his wife's or girlfriend's responsibility to correct the other women because of her insecurity. A woman who corrects the sinner for her own wellbeing, is driven to clear the path of 'beautiful, sinful women' so her husband will not be tempted to gaze. This is the devil's way of bringing hostility, jealousy, envy, strife, and wrongdoing into the body of Christ. Now, imagine Christians correcting each other. What unsaved person wants to become a member of Christ, or who would want to stay a Christian when they are always being asked to change their sinning ways?

In 2018, while still working with the school district, we had volunteers helping in the Parent Room. They would assist with classroom or workroom projects. A young couple often offered their help, for which I was beyond grateful! The young couple were in their 20's and did not seem compatible from my point of view. The boyfriend Raven was a proud Atheist and his "religious" girlfriend Amber seemed to find some pleasure in his lifestyle. He received a lot of attention because of his tattoos, and she enjoyed the shock on people's faces. Amber would announce his belief in Satan when introducing him. With his upside-down cross, gothic style, and Lucifer tattooed on his leg, his belief was obvious.

I had the privilege to speak to him when we met and I assigned them their work. As I laid my eyes on Raven, the Lord revealed His love for him. I embraced him with love and comfort, and this appeared to confuse him. Raven seemed to think he needed to declare his love for Satan. I explained to him how Jesus loves him as much as He loves me, and that there is nothing he could do to remove that love. This man began to cry. Amber was out of the room at that time. I knew God set it up that way so he could show Raven what God wanted him to know. God told me that Amber would only hold him back from receiving God's Truth. The Lord told me to share with him a spiritual video that I had. As I told him about this video, he put on a smirk, but I continued to tell him God's Truth. I also made him promise to watch it while he was alone. (This was to avoid Amber discouraging him.) He hesitated but then promised he would. A few days later, he called me to tell say he had watched it and liked it. This guy had so many questions! I loved it!

The school year was now over. I did not see him anymore, and I did not expect to hear from him again. Then one day, he called to say he wanted to accept Jesus! God is always on the move. He felt ashamed about his tattoos, but I told him that God will open doors for many testimonies to come. He needed to decide whether he removes them or not.

> **"I have not called the righteous but sinners to repentance." Luke 5:32 and "…God's kindness is meant to lead you to repentance?"**
> **Romans 2:4**

God is always on the move, but as Christians we need to be ready and willing to hear what our next move will be in this world. Judging others based on where they're at in life is not the way to witness Christ. It is the goodness of God that brings people to repentance.

> "Love is patient and kind; love does not envy or boast; *it is not arrogant or rude.* It does not *insist on its own way;* it is not *irritable or resentful;* it does not *rejoice at wrong doing,* but rejoices with the truth."
>
> 2 Corinthians 13: 4-6

"GOD IS EITHER A LIAR, OR MAN
KEEPS MAKING EXCUSES FOR
STAYING IGNORANT."

———————

ROSEMARY V. CANTU

FINAL THOUGHT

Come now, you who say, "Today or tomorrow
we will go into such and such a town and spend
a year there and trade and make a profit"—
yet you do not know what tomorrow will bring.
What is your life? For you are a mist that appears
for a little time and then vanishes. Instead you
ought to say, "If the Lord wills, we will live and
do this or that."

James 14:13-17

Do not worry about tomorrow. Instead, pray if it is the Lord's will to move, or to do this or that. When you rent a movie, sometimes at the end the producers will show two or three different scenarios of how the movie could have ended. When viewing each possible ending, the original movie is always better.

The Lord showed me this when I was reading these verses. God has already planned our paths, but it is through our obedience that we fulfill our purpose in life, which is His favor in us in Christ. Each choice we make determines our direction. He puts his will before you in order to live according to his vision.

> *"For it is God who works in you, both to will and to work for his good pleasure."*
> **Phil 2:13**

If we make the wrong choice, He will not forsake us but continue to guide us in the right direction.